I'M BREATHING, SO IT'S A GOOD DAY

Reflections from My Life as a Father, a Minister, and a Chaplain

Eric B. Verhulst

Dedication

To all who wrestle with God and life, but continue to
keep the faith.

Table of Contents

Introduction

I've been in the ministry now for 25 years, roughly half of that time as a Navy Chaplain, the other half serving two different congregations on the prairies. And I've been married for going on 32 years. Over those years, I've recorded some anecdotes and written some poems reflecting my life. You'll find selections from those writings here, interspersed with aphorisms and one-liners I've coined or collected along the way.

I do use abbreviations in the poems. To keep the meter, read them out. KIA, for example, should be heard as "kay eye ay".

1MC=Main Ship's Channel–broadcasts to entire ship
BAS=Battalion Aid Station
IED=Improvised Explosive Device
KIA=Killed In Action
MIA=Missing In Action
POW=Prisoner Of War
RP=Religious Program Specialist (enlisted chaplain support)

Finally, there are two cartoons, one just before, one just after the War Poems section. Both arise out of my experience in the military – the one an actual event. My thanks to Ms. Alustriel Day for drawing them for me.

FAMILY MAN

BEDTIME STORIES

Bedtime was always an experience when my kids were younger. Around 8 pm, I or my wife would say "Bedtime, kids!" Those words started off a whole series of events.

First, there was the "one last thing" that needed doing before hopping off to the bathroom to brush teeth. And, of course, the route to the bathroom was the most indirect available. The toothbrushes came out and toothpaste was applied - though not necessarily just to the toothbrush. Toothpaste was applied to the sink, to each other, to the floors, cupboards, and counter as well. Then it was into pajamas and off to find stories.

The children were not dumb. They'd take their sweet time picking one out, even though they really knew the story they were looking for when they headed for the shelf - the longest one they could find. But I had ways of editing stories that were too long.

I'd sit in my chair while the kids made a big project of climbing onto my lap. All three of them fit in those days, even while they squirmed around trying to get comfortable. The first story would come out - Curious George Gets a Medal - and I'd begin.

"Ralph was a curious hippopotamus-"
"NOOOO! George!"
"George?"
"Yes!"

7

"OK. George was a curious hippopot-"

"NOOOO! Monkey!"

"I thought you said his name was George?"

"George is a monkey!"

"Aahh. I get it now. George was a curious monkey..."

The stories now read, there are hugs & kisses all 'round - and we mustn't forget the dog, mind you. Then off to bed at last. In the movies, children climb willingly into neatly made beds, cuddling a favorite teddy bear or some such. In real life, nothing about the room or the bed is neat. There are several dozen stuffed animals cluttering the bed which need to be moved just to make room for the child. Then the books need to be ferreted out or I can see the headline - CHILD BLINDED BY CAT IN HAT! In my daughter's bed various Barbie parts, clothes, etc. would be stashed while my son's bed would look like a used car lot for Hot Wheels or Matchbox. At last we say prayers and tuck them in.

Five minutes later, sitting in the front room with a cup of tea or soda, watching TV with our feet up after a long day, the inevitable would start. "Thump." "Thump-thump." "Thumpthumpthumpthump." Somebody's coming down the stairs. "Patpatpatpatpatpatpat." Somebody's running across the kitchen. And then they would burst into the living room with a toe-nail that needed clipping or waving underpants like a pinwheel because he needs help getting them on again. Or the sentimental excuse - "I just wanted to give you another kiss." I'd pretend to be angry and they'd pretend to pout, but this, too, was part of the nightly ritual.

It's all gone, now. The kids grew up and grew busier. They read their own stories now and sometimes I'm in bed before they are. Maybe someday they'll read me a story.

*****

Books about raising kids can be helpful. Just remember the kids have not read them.

MUD

Spring has apparently sprung. More than any other season of the year, I think I like spring best. Fall is a close second, but spring is still my favorite. Spring is the most hopeful season. Babies - human and otherwise - are born in the spring. Fields, lawns and gardens are planted in the spring. People get married in the spring more often than any other season. Almost every birthday or anniversary in my family falls between March and June - though a few decided they had to be different and were born in July. Spring is when people come outside and greet their neighbors again. Spring, in other words, is when people celebrate life. I think maybe we should start each year with the first day of Spring rather than January - make March 20th New Year's Day.

Spring is also a time when it rains. Folks at the university tell us sometimes that our ancestors crawled out of the mud millions of years ago. I don't know about that. I wasn't there and I reckon the professor types who say it weren't there, either. But I do know that every spring our descendants crawl back into the mud. Mud is so delightfully dirty. I watch my children play in it and remember the sheer joy of swerving off to stomp in a puddle - quickly, before mom can finish saying not to. Or I would take my shoes off and feel the mud ooze between my toes. Then I'd walk backwards on the sidewalk so I could see my footprints on the (formerly) clean cement. Even when I was in high school, there was something deliciously rebellious about riding my bike through the puddles and having the tires spatter mud all up my back. I don't have to coach my children in the joys of mud, though. There's something about children and mud that creates a natural, mutual attraction.

I'm older now, and concerned with laundry, keeping clothes clean, not making extra work or ruining good clothes, and generally behaving properly. I keep my shoes on these days and only rarely do I ride a bike. But I still like to drive my car through puddles and if you watch me closely, you may just see me out for a walk stomping in puddles with my son. Sometimes being adult is just more trouble than its worth.

*****

A zero-defect requirement produces a zero-honesty response.

FIRST FRONTIER

I always get a kick out of the opening sequence on the old *Star Trek* series - "Space, a final frontier..." Are these guys going to distant stars or just driving west of the Missouri in North Dakota? Actually, there's plenty of space east of the Missouri, for that matter. From the time when our grandparents first came to settle this land, space has been one of the big draws of the prairies. You might have space in Ohio too, but there are so many trees, you can't tell. Here on the prairies, you can crest a hill which may be all of 200 feet and see for miles - and see nothing moving but insects, a few birds, and grass.

All this space is good for raising things - corn, wheat, cattle and kids. I remember talking to someone in a city about dogs. "I don't want a big dog here in the city. It just isn't fair to the dog. A dog needs room to run," he said. I don't disagree with him, but I got to thinking. Dogs aren't the only ones who need room to run and be curious. Children do, too. It's part of growing up.

Look at a child, for instance, when he first learns to walk. A thousand things are opened up to him, and he must investigate them all. He can crawl up on the couch and see what happens to his favorite ball when he drops it behind the furniture. He can walk over to the table and pull the plate over the edge without having to let go of his bottle. He can reach up for things on the desk and skedaddle before anyone knows it was him. He can experiment with sneaking up on the dog and falling on him. The world becomes so much more exciting and

12

enticing to him once he can walk. Once he's able to chase and catch a frog or snake, bound off after a rabbit, or wade into a field of grass that's a foot over his head the age of discovery has well and truly begun. They need space for this.

In a city, you've got to keep the kids fenced in, leashed to your yard. People in cities don't have a lot of room to call their own and they get very protective of what little they have. Traffic, even in residential areas, is often too heavy to let the kids run. So kids turn to TV and video games to satisfy their thirst for novelty. You know what new things they'll discover there - and it isn't snakes and frogs. I'm glad I was able to let my children run free on the prairies where there's plenty of space – their first frontier.

*****

The sole legitimate purpose of authority is to serve those over whom it is exercised.

THE COMFORTS OF LIFE

Children, for some reason, seem to enjoy the idea of roughing it. They like camping. They like running around outside. They like eating things that have been cooked over a fire - not a fake fire like a burner on an oven, but a real fire. For several thousand years, human beings have been striving to achieve the comforts which we now enjoy - indoor plumbing, refrigerators, ovens, washers, beds, central heating, and other such things. Slaving away in order to have wood enough for the winter or trekking to the outhouse on a hot summer day were irritating necessities of our grandfathers' time. But to a three-year-old, relieving yourself in an outhouse with 3000 flies hovering about is an adventure. Nevertheless, fools that we are, we parents work hard to provide our children and grandchildren with these conveniences.

I was walking past my daughter's room one night when she was about seven. I had tucked her into bed, yet there she lay, on the floor in her sleeping bag. "Why are you on the floor?" I asked, rather stupidly I might add.

"Because I want to be here," she answered, stating the obvious. In school your teachers will tell you not to be afraid to ask questions because there is no such thing as a stupid question. Either your teacher is lying to you or she never had parents. Parents have a real knack for asking stupid questions.

Asking the question I should have asked the first time, I say, "Why do you want to be on the floor?"

14

"I don't know." I don't know either. I spend $400 on a bedroom set for her. I spend $50 for a comforter for the bed, $20 for a bedskirt, and another $50 for sheets and pillows – several hundred dollars to give her the comforts of a good life, and she is sleeping on the floor. No, I really do not know why she wants to sleep on the floor and now I also don't know why I spent that much money for a bed she doesn't use. But what am I going to do? She's sleeping on the floor.

I walked past my son's bedroom. His sleeping bag was on his bed. He was on the floor looking at books by flashlight under a couple of blankets.

There are times when it's best to just keep walking.

*****

Don't confuse education with intelligence. There are lots of highly educated idiots.

THOUGHTS ON A LONG WINTER

It's shaped up into a long winter and, as I write, the snow is falling yet again. Sometimes I think my son is the only person in the area regularly thanking God for the snow. At every meal, "Thank you for this food, thank you for this day, thank you for the snow..." I suppose some of the kids who get out of school because of the snow thank God at the time, but from the sound of their complaints, even they are getting tired of snow and cold all the time. I know I am.

Snow is hard to appreciate as an adult. For most of us, it's either ignored or it's a problem. On those rare occasions when we have time to go skiing, then we appreciate it - but we'd appreciate it a lot more if the snow would stay on the ski slopes and off our sidewalks and roads. We adults are busy with the work that must be done, the places that must be gotten to, and all the responsibilities of life. When snow covers the yard, blows into the machinery, and almost right through the eight layers of coats and shirts I'm wearing, it makes those chores take all that much longer, in addition to adding a few more chores like moving that snow out of the way. When it drifts up on the road, it slows or stops the milk truck from getting through, stops me from getting to town for parts, gas, groceries, or a cup of coffee. It may even stop the mail. "Neither rain nor snow nor sleet nor hail..." but a 7-foot drift will. Stops him cold.

But there is a certain beauty to the even slope of the drifts, the perfect curves of snow stretching tentacles across the road. There is something mysterious about a white haze of snow blowing over the roads which looks like a thin sheet in constant motion. The almost claustrophobic feel you get when you drive through a canyon of snow piled up by the plows almost twice as high as your pickup. And if I let myself relax, enjoy the enforced tranquility of a few days shut in by snow I, too, can find myself thanking God for snow. While I'm at it, I think I'll also thank God for central heating.

*****

It's another lovely day in paradise — and if only we were there instead of here.

HOMEWORK

"Dad, can you help me with my homework?"

"Sure, dear. What's up?"

"I've got to get this Science Project to get ready and I picked 'Cheese Production' but I don't know where to look for stuff. Do we have any books about cheese?"

I've got a lot of books, covering a wide array of topics from science fiction to a history of mathematics, from fantasy to Dooyeweerdian philosophy, and other esoteric topics. But I don't have anything on cheese. Regrettably, I tell her this and suggest, "We can go to the library and see what they have, and I'm sure there's stuff on the Web about it, so there's lots of information we can get on it. What were you going to do with this topic of yours?"

"Well, I was sort of, like, going to, you know, like how is cheese made and stuff."

"How cheese is made and stuff," I repeat. "Well, what is the assignment?" She hands me a pack of a half-dozen sheets stapled together, outlining the project. As I get to the end of this document, a date appears. "This is due on Monday!"

"I know."

"It's Thursday night! Tomorrow you're having friends over. Saturday you've got a youth group outing. Sunday's church. When, exactly, did you propose doing this?"

"Tonight - that's why I'm showing it to you."

"When did you get this assignment?"

"I don't know - a while ago."

"The library's already closed!"

"It is? I thought they stayed open late."

"Yeah, but not 10 o'clock late! You've got the laptop, right?"

"Yes."

"Well, let's locate some web site for you, but next time start on it a little earlier for Pete's sake!"

As I begin looking up web sites, my older son comes in. "Dad, can you help me with my homework? I've got this Science Project to get ready and I picked..."

*****

Making children happy is not a parental responsibility. Training them to be responsible adults is.

DINNER WITH SMALL CHILDREN

Dinner with small children is always an adventure, or should I simply say it is a challenge? When we were first married, we could sit down together at the table, enjoy a pleasant meal and quiet conversation. We would discuss plans for the remainder of the week, the day at work, a book or magazine article one of us had read or some TV show we had seen. It was generally a subdued and relaxing experience. Not anymore. The natural competitive instincts of children coupled with their almost frightening honesty and the tendency to substitute volume for reasoned argument all combine to make the meal so much more challenging - and consequently, less relaxing - than it used to be.

The first course, served as soon as everyone is at the table, if not before, is an argument over whose turn it is to pray first. Once that's settled, one or the other invariably accuses somebody of opening their eyes, forgetting that they would have to violate the same rule in order to find out. Then the actual food is brought out to be greeted by a chorus of "Yuck!" The problem with this (from a child's perspective, anyway) is that the children have now agreed on something. This is anathema. The first rule of a three-year-old at dinner is that if your sister says something, you must immediately disagree with it. If she likes it, you don't. If she doesn't, you do. As soon as they realize they have agreed to dislike it, there is a race to see who can be first to claim an undying passion for creamed gravy on Brussels sprouts or whatever else is set before

20

them. I have honestly heard my children arguing at dinner as to who liked something first. It is truly amazing.

The next step is to sit and stare at the food until it's cold and then complain that it is cold. I tend to be less than sympathetic to their cries and try to bribe them with dessert or a favorite video or something to inspire their appetites. My son, however, hasn't quite figured out that what I want is for him to go through *all* the steps of eating - put it in the mouth, chew it, swallow it, next bite, and so on. As far as he is concerned, once it's in the mouth, it's eaten. Soon his cheeks are bulging like a chipmunk's, half chewed, salivated vegetables oozing out between his teeth despite his best efforts. But worst of all, he now tries to speak. "Ahh d(food spewing forth)one. Caaa ahh wat Pohnga nahh?" which, after the mess is cleaned up and the translation is completed, means "I'm done. Can I watch Pongo (101 Dalmatians) now?"

I was mentioning this to my mother the other day and she seemed not the least bit concerned with the difficulties I face as a parent. Quite the contrary. She seemed almost gleeful. Why is that?

*****

Never underestimate the ability of the human mind to rationalize evil.

STUPID FIGHTS

"You better go down and talk to your children."

Uh-oh. Whenever she says "your children" they're screwing up. "Why? What's up?"

"I don't know. I just heard a lot of yelling and then I think Roger hit Dana."

OK. I go downstairs and find my children - the older two - in the kitchen. They are glaring sullenly at each other and I see tears in one pair of eyes. I pull out a chair from the table, sit down, and ask "What's going on?"

"We were supposed to be cleaning the kitchen," the older one begins. "And after we'd swept and cleaned the floor we were putting back the chairs and I put the chair here and Roger took it and said it doesn't go there and put it over here so I took it back and put it where I had it and then he hit me and it's not fair because it doesn't matter and I put the chair here..." She is obviously feeling very much ill-used by her brother. So I look to Roger. "Is this true?" I ask. He just sort of nods, not daring to speak and hardly daring to look in my direction.

I look at them incredulously. "Let me get this straight. I see five chairs here. They are, for all intents and purposes, identical chairs. And I have two children fighting over which of two identical chairs goes with which of two identical places at the table. Am I the only person here who thinks this is incredibly stupid?"

The younger one starts to speak to defend himself. I cut him off..

22

"Dana. You just told me that it doesn't matter. If it doesn't matter, and Roger wants the chair at this place instead of that place, why does that bother you? And Roger. All the chairs are the same! Do you really think one chair goes here and another goes there? How can you tell? And yet I have two children - whose teachers mistakenly believe are very smart - coming to blows over where IDENTICAL CHAIRS GO AT A KITCHEN TABLE!! I'm sorry. There is no other word for it. This is dumb. I mean, this is incredible, record-shattering, mind-blowing stupidity."

Though Dana tries mightily to continue feeling abused, mistreated and aggrieved, she can no longer suppress a giggle. Roger looks over at her and starts to smile. They both look at their toes as they admit, "Yeah. It is kinda stupid."

"No, it's more than 'kinda' stupid. It's *really* stupid. So do me a favor and stop being stupid."

*****

Girl, stop bugging your brother.
Boy, stop being bugged.

MUSIC LESSONS

My son lay on the bed, tears welling in his eyes. One could hardly comprehend the depths of his agony. What he was about to do was little short of sheer torture. He wondered aloud if Amnesty International was aware of such cruelty, would they not act? Given Amnesty International's history, lumping together the trivial and the horrible in a single bundle as they do, I might be in trouble. But I will dare their wrath this evening. My son will still practice his baritone.

After I finished this conversation, my wife informed me that our daughter was of the opinion that the only reason we made her take piano lessons was because we hate her. So I called her over.

"I understand, my darling daughter, that you think your mother hates you."

"Yeah," she said sullenly, but firmly.

"You are mistaken."

"Oh?" She raised her eyebrow, kind of like Spock.

"Yes. Your mother does not hate you. Over the last several months, your mother has been of a mind to stop hauling you to the piano studio, fighting with you to practice, and generally struggle with this whole issue. She is willing to let you stop. I have been the one to say, 'No. The little tart is going to play the piano.' You see, it's not your mother who hates you. I hate you. That's why you are taking piano lessons."

She just looked at me.

24

Yesterday was Tuesday - piano lesson time. As I pushed the kids to get ready, I told her, "You know, of course, that the only reason I'm leaving my warm, comfortable house, missing an opportunity to enjoy a family meal, play on my computer, read a book, and go to bed early in order to take you to piano lessons is nothing other than sheer, unadulterated, inexplicable malice."

If looks could kill...

*****

Anyone who believes children are innocent hasn't spent enough time with children.

TEENSPEAK

Language is a beautiful thing. To hear the sounds of the human voice rationalized, conveying meaning, channeling thought, or playfully teasing itself is astounding. Whether it be the epic, high art of Shakespeare or Milton, or the equally epic, gritty humor of Mark Twain, it is a joy to hear the art of language practiced well. Then to ponder how many different systems of language there are - it is truly awesome. I have had occasion to study several languages and have at least a nodding acquaintance with them, though I'd hardly say I'm fluent. And whether it is German, Italian, Navajo, Spanish, Latin, Greek, Hebrew or, of course, English, there is art and order in the sounds uttered.

Then there is "teenagese". I have striven to convey this sense of awe and wonder at the power of language to my children. My children got in the car the other day when I picked them up at school. My daughter began relating some events that had occurred in class.

"And then, like, Mallory, like, she was saying, like, you know, dude! And Lizzy was, like, you can't mean that, I mean, really! Like Brittany was, you know, like trying to get this thing out of the like, you know, the thingie on her desk and it was, like, so funny!"

In the space of fifteen minutes, I counted some 74 "like's", 27 "you know's" and 13 "thing" or "thingie" variations. There were also several "dude's" "really's" "so's" "and then's," not to mention the archaic "cool" and "wow" tossed in to keep things going. My daughter is not normally the most loquacious of my children. For her to speak steadily for 15 minutes indicates a degree of excitement and interest rarely seen. But other than the general understanding that somehow Mallory, Lizzy, Brittany, and my daughter were involved in some humorous anecdote surrounding their teacher, she was utterly incomprehensible. At least I thought so. But just to be sure, I tested the hypothesis.

"Son. Do you know what she's talking about?"

"Sure, Dad. It's like this girl in her class, you know, Mallory - she like..."

I surrendered.

"Like, sure, son. It's not like, you know, I need you to repeat the whole story, dude. I was, like, just wanting to know, like, if you, like, really understood your sister."

*****

Spend all your time thinking about yourself and eventually you're the only one thinking about you.

ROAD TRIP

Travelling with children is always an experience to be anticipated with more than a little sense of foreboding. This is even more the case when the children are preschoolers. On the wide open prairies, such forbidding experiences are necessarily common, however.

We went to visit grandpa and grandma last week during the break in school for teachers' conferences. My son thought this was great. He knew it would be a long trip, so managed to hold off as far as Ellendale before asking if we were there yet. We weren't. But we only had 7 more hours to drive by that point. Try explaining to a preschooler just what an hour is. For that matter, try explaining it to a teenager. We also had seven more hours of "Are we there yet?" This doesn't bother me, though. What bothers is that soon after they start asking if we've arrived, the children get bored. They've played with the limited number of toys you've brought along well beyond the endurance of their attention spans. They don't care to watch the prairie roll by - to them one patch of grass looks pretty much like another. And the only songs they know are "Jesus Loves Me" and "100 Bottles of Beer on the Wall". I'm not going to start that one. So the only thing left for the little folks is to start fighting.

It wouldn't be so bad if all they would do is fight, but little children don't fight by themselves. They fight by saying "Mooooommmmmm. She won't let me look out the window." "Daaaaddddd. He keeps pulling my braid!" And on it goes. Mooommmm. Daaaadddd.

28

I fixed them, though. "Dddaaannnaaa! Mommy won't share her crossword puzzle with me!" My wife caught on. "Rrrooogggeeerrr! Daddy won't let me drive!" So they answered us the way they've become accustomed to us answering them. "Daddy, if you don't let Mommy drive, I'm going to have to spank you! Do you want me to stop this car, Daddy?" It all sounded rather silly when it was the other one saying it. Pretty soon they were laughing so hard at themselves, at me and at my wife that they couldn't fight anymore. But I got to thinking. When you look around at the rolling hills, the endless fields, the clouds sailing lazily through the sky - the same sky, the same clouds, the same fields and hills which have been seen by countless generations, when you think that mothers and fathers have been trying to keep kids entertained on long trips for as long as there have been parents and children, and then consider what it is that we're so worked up about today, one is struck by how trivial our fights can be - as trivial as who gets to sit next to the window in the car. And the answer is obvious. If you're going to enjoy a long trip with the kids, you can't take them or yourself too seriously and frankly, if you're going to enjoy a long life, you can't take them or yourself too seriously.

*****

Everything until you're forty is just education.

IT'S KINDA NEAT

We didn't really talk much about it, at least, not with each other. We both knew the reality – I was in the Navy, assigned to a ship, and that meant I was leaving. We talked about it with the kids, mentioning the date, taking time to do a few things together as a family. We wanted them prepared for the coming deployment and kids can take it much better if they know what's coming. Except for birthday presents, children don't take surprises well. Mine don't, anyway.

The day finally arrived and I buried myself in last-minute preparations – making sure I had whatever I might need for uniforms, civilian clothes, books, and so on. We were leaving early, so it was the night before our actual departure that she drove me to the pier. The kids helped me bring my gear aboard and I walked with them back out to the car. We tried our best to act as if this was normal, no big deal, but there was a quietness about the kids that belied our efforts. Neither I nor my wife is given to emotional displays, so a simple embrace, a kiss, and good-bye ended the ceremony. I shut the car door, traded a few jokes with my older boy through the open window; my youngest saluted, so I returned it; said good-bye one more time and started toward the gate at the head of the pier.

I was trying not to feel, to be quite frank. If I were to feel anything, I'd feel depressed and I couldn't afford that – if the Chaplain's depressed, we're in trouble, right? On the other hand, who likes leaving his wife and kids for six months (or more)? In spite of these sentiments, I was both proud and grateful. I was going to sea. This is what sailors do and it is why I joined the Navy. Like my father before me, I would deploy on a large, gray, metal thing called a ship. It made no difference that he deployed on the USS NEOSHO (AO-143) in '67 and I on the USS GEORGE WASHINGTON (CVN-73) thirty-three years later. What mattered is that we were both U.S. Navy sailors. Neither of us will make the history books since the supply of "Bull" Halsey's, Horatio Nelson's, David Farragut's, and John Paul Jones' is rather limited. Even so, both of us are part of a 240-year-plus tradition involving hundreds of thousands of nameless U.S. Navy sailors going to sea in service to this country. I was – am – honored to be a part of this salt-water brotherhood.

A couple days before I left on deployment, I was discussing where I'd go next with my wife. My daughter was listening and she asked, "Is that a ship?" I told her, "No, but there are ships assigned to the squadron and I'll get to go out on them sometimes." She looked disappointed. "What's wrong?"

"It's just that it's kinda neat, you being on a ship." As I crossed the quarterdeck and headed below to my rack, it occurred to me how right she was. I am grateful, proud, and honored that, long after I crossed the quarterdeck to leave the ship, both my now grown sons have joined the naval service to take their turn at the watch. I doubt that either of them will make the history books any more than I or my father did, but we may sleep more soundly because they and thousands like them are, or soon will be, guarding distant seas and nearer shores. As my daughter said, it's kinda neat.

*****

Remember, you've never been your parents' age, but they were once your age.

THE JOYS OF LANGUAGE

Profanity is universally acclaimed to be a bad thing.
And at the extremes, where it is currently practiced, I'd
have to agree. I tried valiantly while on board ship to
teach sailors a wide scope of adjectives so they would not
be limited to those indicating fornication - particularly
fornicating mothers. Language that is over-used soon
loses its force or meaning. We find that to be the case in
advertising. Every sale is "THIS WEEK ONLY!!" but we
all know there will be a nearly identical sale starting the
day after this one ends. The phrase becomes meaningless.
Used sparingly, there are times when it is appropriate to
associate certain behaviors with the infernal regions. For
example, "What the HELL are you doing?!?!?!?"

I learned profanity from my mother, and she often
asked me that question. At times she would let me know
that certain objects were also bound for the lake of fire,
too, as in "Move that damned bike of yours out of the
driveway so I can park my car!" She was meticulously
careful to leave God out of it - she did not want to
actually take God's name in vain. But she was not above
telling me that my room strongly resembled fecal matter.
My mother did try to restrict her use of these words to
special occasions. She was very aware that overuse
would render the words pointless.

My mother also wanted to make a theological point
with us when she used these words or phrases. They are
indelibly linked in my mind with the use of long, flat
wooden objects on my posterior. Apparently she felt it

her duty to ensure the relationship between hell and pain was firmly embedded in my mind - and behind. If I could not be coaxed into heaven, I might at least be driven there.

We were visiting my parents over the July 4th weekend and my mother took my daughter shopping. They frequently do the "girls day out" thing when we visit. Later, when we were going as a family to visit some college friends of mine, my daughter said to me, "Grandma drives like you do, Dad."

"What do you mean? It's not surprising, of course. I learned to drive from her so I suppose it better to say that I drive like her."

"Well," she said. "I don't know about the driving itself, but you use the same words."

*****

Looking out for #1 is a recipe for coming in last.

34

THE LIST

Summer is full upon us now. It's getting warmer.
The kids are home from school. And the round of visits
to family, summer camps, etc., etc., is heating up.

My wife and I both work, and that means frequently
the kids are home. Kids at home without the parents there
are kids who will use their time frivolously. The great
god Nintendo beckons them to its 27" diagonal measure
altar where they will hear the sacred stories of Donkey
Kong or Rogue Squadron or Mario. There are some
1,300 books in my house and they haven't read them all -
not that they will, but that Calvin & Hobbes anthology
certainly is tempting. To avoid these evils, Barb leaves a
list of chores and responsibilities covering laundry,
dishes, lunch, vacuuming, dog walks, practicing piano,
and so on.

So yesterday, I got home and found the family room
to be an absolute mess while three children sat enraptured
in front of the television, blissfully unaware of either my
presence or the mess. I stood there for a few minutes just
watching them in amazement. "How can they be so
blind?" I thought. So I "ahemed" loudly. One heard and
notified the others who said "Hi Daddy" without taking
their eyes off the set.

"Why aren't these clothes folded and taken care of?"

The inevitable answer followed. "What clothes?"

"The clothes scattered all over the living room! Open
your eyes!"

"These clothes?"

"YES. THESE CLOTHES! Why aren't they taken care of?"

"Oh! Those clothes. Well, they weren't on the list."

*****

Nobody needs cable television.

GIFTS FOR DAD

I picked my kids up from school the other day, slipped in behind a large vehicle - although, I drive a GEO Metro so every other car on the road seems like a large vehicle - and saw three "PROUD PARENT OF AN HONOR ROLL STUDENT AT_____" stickers on the back.

I thought it, and I thought it aloud. "I should get a bumper sticker that reads 'SLIGHTLY EMBARRASSED PARENT OF AN IDIOT.'"

According to the parenting books, those sorts of comments supposedly damage a child's self-esteem forever and have disastrous consequences. Maybe my kids will all grow up to be crack-heads, ne'er-do-wells, bums, and so on. My children, however, are quite familiar with Dad's bursts of cynicism and sarcasm. Almost in unison they asked, "Which one of us gets to be the idiot? Can I be the idiot?"

"I'm sure each of you can do that job. I think you all have the requisite gifts."

The oldest one speaks up, "I'm the oldest - I get to be the first idiot."

"Yeah," says the next. "I get my turn right after you."

My youngest says, "That would be a good Father's Day present. Are you going to get one for your Dad, too?"

*****

GOING OUT WITH CHILDREN

A lot of people think BC means "Before Christ." For us, it means "Before Children." I remember life before children. Barb and I could get up 30 minutes before we had to leave, shower, breakfast, dress, and be headed out the driveway a few minutes early. We could go for walks that meant actually walking. We could eat a dinner and converse. Then we had children.

I love my children. But I think the only thing my daughter has done in less than thirty minutes is think about what she is going to wear. Actually *deciding* what she is going to wear, then putting it on takes a minimum of an hour. If she's going to shower - which requires extensive hair rituals - add another hour.

My sons can act in less than thirty minutes, but they can't stay focused for more than two. When getting ready for school, we have to ban all reading material, including handouts, books, cereal boxes, bread bags (they read the ingredients) - anything with words on it has to be put away. Even so, they manage to distract each other with toys, stories, jokes, and general nonsense so that when I do check in on them, I find one half in a shirt, the other with just one pants leg on, and both of them laughing wildly as they describe with their hands or feet some incident they saw or imagined.

We plan an hour and a half to get ready now, but we only tell the kids we have an hour, otherwise they'd take two.

38

As we head for the restaurant, my son sees something shiny on the driveway and goes to grab it. "I was looking for this paperclip! It must have fallen off my papers when we were getting out of the car yesterday."

"Why were you looking for a paperclip? We have plenty in the desk drawer."

"I know, but this one was with the papers and when I got to my room it wasn't." And that explains...what? But I'm reluctant to push the issue. It's only 20 feet from the front door to the car. It takes 10 minutes to get everybody shepherded across this expanse.

At the restaurant, the two boys start discussing how closely their food resembles various bodily excretions. Efforts to quell this line of conversation only lead to worse topics. My wife and I can't really talk because we are constantly saying, "Don't slurp. Sit up. CAREFUL! I don't care what he said, don't kick your brother!" Inevitably, somebody knocks over a beverage. If we're lucky, it's got a lid on it, but drinks *will* be knocked over.

My wife looks at me., "You know, it's a nice gesture to take me out for dinner on Mother's Day, but cooking would probably be easier."

*****

God gives us teenagers so we'll know what he feels like being our Father.

DAD SHOPPING

"I hate shopping. It takes forever, you try on a couple dozen outfits, nothing fits right and you end up going home after a whole day tired and you still haven't gotten anything."

What makes that statement so amazing is that I didn't say it. My daughter did. Being the sympathetic father, I asked her what happened.

"We-"

"Who's 'we'?"

"Me and Mom. We went to the mall and checked out Hecht's and Penny's and Dillards and some of the boutiques and then we went to Target and Wal-Mart and K-Mart and Sears. We spent all day Saturday - TWICE."

"And you saw nothing you liked?"

"I don't know. I just got sick of it."

"Well, dear, I have a solution," I announced. She looked at me rather skeptically. "Tell you what. Tomorrow I'll take you 'Dad-Shopping'. Before you object, I will guarantee you that we will be gone less than 2 hours, including a leisurely lunch, and you will come back with a minimum of two outfits."

"Dayid!" There's something about the way a teenager says the word 'Dad', by the way. It's two syllables, not one, and at once conveys skepticism, irritation, frustration, and outright disbelief.

The next day we went out to the mall. We went into one store. We went straight to the Petits section (she's only 12 - that's petit, right?). She followed me,

40

reluctantly, as I strode through the clothes. Whenever I'd stop, she'd put her weight on one foot, tilt her head to the left, and give me this exasperated look which veritably shouted "DAYID!" I ignored it. I held up a dress to her. "Hmmm. Looks about right. Hang on to that one." A few seconds later, another. "Naah, won't do. Not your style." Next rack. "That'll do. Hang on to that one."

"Dayid!"

"What?"

"I wanted a denim skirt, not these. They're too dressy."

"You need something like that, don't you?"

"Yeah."

"Nuff said. But I think I saw some denim skirts over there." We marched on over. Picked one off the rack, held it up. "That'll fitcha. Need a top to go with it, though." Over to the tops. "Naah. Won't do. Aaaah! That's the ticket. Here you go. Dressing rooms are over there."

She gave me a look that would kill a horse, but went over to the dressing rooms. After seeing her in the various outfits, we rejected one, bought the other two, and headed to the food court. Elapsed time: 45 minutes - and most of that was driving to the mall.

"See, that's Dad-shopping."

*****

MIXED FEELINGS

This is the first year I've taken advantage of some of the freebies area businesses offer veterans on Veterans' Day. I must say, I have mixed feelings about it.

You know, there's that old saw that gets a fair bit of sarcastic treatment: "My salary is pay enough." But the truth is, my salary, and the benefits that went along with it, was pay enough. I knew what I was doing and I loved the doing of it. I am honored that I had the privilege of serving.

Then there's the fact that, while I did get shot at and certainly saw enough incoming mortar and rocket fire to satisfy my taste for it, others endured and did so much more. In the first place, all the people who shot at me missed. In the second place, I was the chaplain. What that means is, I had 1,000 guardian angels wearing desert digital camouflage and keeping a sharp eye out. I never once worried about myself, because there were 1,000 strong men, well-armed who were worried about my safety. Marines take care of their chaplains and docs, let me tell you. Serving such men is all the honor I could ever want. It is not I who need to be thanked, but them.

And yet, I am also proud to be able to say that I did my duty. I've mentioned it before and it is true. I volunteered, and then volunteered again for deployments into combat theaters whenever I could - because that's where they need a chaplain, not at home where clergy are a dime-a-dozen. I earned no bronze or silver stars, no combat V, no Navy Cross. I simply did my duty, to my family, my country, and my God. A free lunch at Applebee's is not too much gratitude for that, is it?

So I went, and saw this old man eating by himself with a ball cap indicating service in World War II, Korea and Vietnam. My daughter commented on how frequently the call went out for somebody, "Party of one". "Sad," she said, and it is. By all means, give the old man his free lunch on Veterans' Day and say thanks, but what about the other 364 days of the year? Does he eat alone then, too? I pray not.

I was humbled all over again, looking at that ball cap. What have I really done that I have the right to be honored in the same way he is? But the steak was good.

*****

An army of one is very soon a corpse.

EXERCISE

I hate exercise. But I enjoy hating exercise. One of
the things I like about exercising - and there aren't many -
is the privilege of griping about it. This, of course, makes
very little sense, but it is very human. I come back after a
solid workout feeling alert, refreshed, energetic, and just
plain good. In fact, there's very little negative to say
about it, but I hate it just the same. I suppose one of the
things I hate about it is that I have to do it. There's this
perverse, adolescent streak in me that detests just about
anything I have to do. It's a great book, but tell me I must
read it and I'll hate it. It's good for me, but tell me I must
eat it and I'll find it revolting. Exercise is the right thing
to do, and if I allow myself, I like it. But I have to
exercise, so I have to hate it.

I am not alone. More than once I have had a young
shipmate in my office and the essence of his or her
difficulty is that there's always somebody telling them
what they've got to do. They don't like it. They know it
needs to be done. They know it's good for them, good for
the ship, good for the country, good for their families.
But somebody is telling them they must do it, so they
refuse to want it and certainly will not like it. The desire
for a pure, unfettered independence dies hard, no matter
how irrational that desire may be. We want to decide for
ourselves. The lone cowboy, making it out on the wide
open prairie, living as he likes with nobody messing in his
business - this is a truly American dream. Many of our
ancestors came to the U.S. specifically to escape the

44

meddling of others, whether it be meddling in their property, their religion, or their enterprise.

And truth be told, God has had this problem with the human race since he told Adam and Eve they could eat from any tree except this one, here in the middle of the garden. Hundreds of fruit trees, berry bushes, vegetables & fruit - and what did they pick to eat?

Yet for all this, I still hate to exercise. I'm glad the Navy made me do it - gave me something to gripe about and I like to gripe.

*****

Temptation is not a sin – nor is it an excuse.

GOD'S SIDE OF THE BED

Reflections on having to put our dog down,
29 April 2010

We put our dog down yesterday.

She was old – at least 17 and maybe 19 years old. It's hard to tell with mutts you get from the pound just how old they are when you get them unless they're puppies.

Every night, she would walk around the house, going up and down the stairs, checking on everybody to make sure they were in their beds like they were supposed to be. When my wife wasn't there, such as when she was visiting her sister, the dog would come around to my side of the bed and wake me up as if I should be doing something about this obvious problem. She wouldn't be nervous or energetic about it, just quietly insistent that something be done to put the world back the way it should be.

Lately, she's had a lot of trouble navigating those stairs, but she would not let us block them off so she couldn't use them. She insisted on making her rounds. In the midst of those rounds, she would sometimes stop, rather suddenly, and just tremble all over. If she were on a tile or hardwood floor at that point, her legs would frequently slide out from under her and she would fall. Then she'd have to crawl to the carpet or rug or somebody else would have to lift her up so she could stand again. Her hearing was pretty much gone. You'd have to lift up the ear and then speak loudly from just a few inches away if you wanted her to hear you. And she'd

46

have problems related to bowel and bladder function like a lot of elderly dogs.

Then, a few weeks ago, she started bleeding. She bled mostly from her nose and mouth. Sometimes she'd sneeze and the blood would splatter over whatever was in front of her. Often times there would be a puddle of blood by her nose and mouth when she woke up. Along with this, her breathing got more and more difficult and she would plaintively hunt inside the house and out for some place where she could breathe freely. Nights were the worst. She would spend hours thrashing and gasping, trying to get comfortable after she'd made her rounds of the house. My wife thought it didn't bother me because I would still sleep, but I just knew there was nothing I could do about it, so I let it be.

This got worse as time went on. We tried different medications to address it on the off chance that it was something akin to allergies or perhaps some kind of infection, but nothing seemed to change it. It got difficult for her to eat and drink and she was losing weight. Her daily walk was about all she could really enjoy and when it was rainy or foul outside, she would go from door to door hoping the weather would be different at a different exit and she could take her walk. This last week even that was a burden to her no matter how much she tried to enjoy it.

Do we wait for her to go of her own, gasping and wheezing and struggling to the last, or do we make the appointment and accept the inevitable? How much blood

47

do we clean off the carpets and walls and furniture before we accept what must be? How much hope do we put in a few hours when she seems to be doing better? The vet said he'd come out to the house, so we could put her down at home instead of in the sterile and frightening harshness of his examination room. He came out and the dog perked up a bit at this opportunity to defend her home from the intruders, barking and growling at them until she accepted they weren't going to leave. I held her on her blanket, the vet gave her the injection, she relaxed, went limp, and died.

It's hard not to wander the house and check her usual sleeping places. She's not there. Death, even the death of a dog, is just not right. So I think I will go to God's side of the bed and see if he can't do something to put the world back the way it should be.

*****

Sometimes life just sucks.

THIRTY-ONE YEARS

So, 31 years it is. While my wife and I have certainly noted our anniversary each year, we haven't often made a big celebration out of it. In fact, for the first four or five years of our marriage she gave me the same card every year. If she hadn't said anything about it, I'd never have noticed. Of course, for the first four or five years - in fact, I think for the whole 31 years - I don't think I even gave her card. This is not a course of inaction that I'd recommend for husbands as a general rule, but it suits us.

I remember when we were first planning on getting married. Many friends recommended books about it. Most of them were amusing. One of the things Christians frequently get a little squeamish about is sex. This is particularly the case when people talk to clergy. It was known at the time that I would be going to seminary and becoming a clergyman, so they tried to be very careful in the books they gave us. If we'd been "regular" folk, we'd have gotten books about sensual massage or some such. Instead we got books that danced around the topic and invented all sorts of euphemisms. The one I remember best used the phrase "the Marriage Act," which was always capitalized. Generally they did an excellent job of making the whole thing sound frightfully dull, but I'd managed to sneak into a couple of movies when I was a teenager so I knew that wasn't right.

Three years later, when she was pregnant with our first child, she would get asked in shocked, almost horrified tones – often by the same people who gave us

49

those books earlier – "Isn't your husband in seminary?!?"
The other question she got most frequently was also
rather personal. "Was this planned?" I told her she
should answer, "No. We were just screwing around and
somehow this happened." She never would.

Now it's been thirty-one years, two more children,
and homes in Michigan, Indiana, North Dakota, Sicily,
Virginia, North Carolina, and South Dakota - thirty-one
years I've been married to a woman who promised herself
she'd never marry a preacher or a sailor. Thirty-one years
I've been married to a woman who liked being single so
much she planned on staying that way. Ask her and she'll
tell you she doesn't know why she married me. I know.
It was a miracle. And I am eternally grateful to both God
and my wife.

*****

Marriage is not really about love. It's about trust.

"Hey! Chaplain's on deck!
Knock off the #@*&!% swearing!"

WAR POEMS

HOLY SHIT!
Holy shit!
This could be it!
Yeah, I mean,
I'm a Marine,
But if that bullet
Has my name on it
It's still a grave
Even for the brave.

Why not be
This cowardly?
What's to gain
From all this pain?
'Cuz if that bullet
Has my name on it,
It's still a grave
Even for the brave.

Got a baby –
I think that maybe
I could see her –
Not leave this good earth.
Back home in Loveland
Folks won't know it and
It's the same damn grave
Even for the brave.

*****

*I had quite a few conversations with Marines in my
battalion before we went to Iraq in 2004. We all went,
but don't think it was easy, or that we didn't really
understand what we were getting into. We knew we
would not all come back.*

I'm not Jesus. I just work for him.

FIRST KIA

His squad brings him in
This arid tent,
Lay him on the deck.
In the back of his neck
A small, little hole rent
The dust and skin.

Leads a few good men,
Brand new sergeant –
Over him, the doc
Examines and takes stock
Through the blood and scent
Of death we're in.

"Say your prayers, Chaplain."
Hov'ring, knees bent –
An ancient prayerbook,
A life that someone took.
Search for grace and vent,
God hears, hopin'.

I can't help askin',
"Is there a point,
Or just hopeful dreck?
These words won't move a speck
Of dust or blood spent
By these, my men.

"Is there much reason
That I was sent
Here among the dead?
Is it just my own head,
My own discontent
In its season?"

I'd tell them in class
"God doesn't make sense"
Even if he did,
My sergeant still lies dead.
The rest is pretense –
A braying ass.

Read the ancient poem
Then say a prayer.
Doc signs the paper,
And zips up the wrapper.
Briefly we kneel there
Then send him home.

*****

*I remember the first of our battalion to be killed in action.
One wants so much to fix it, to bring hope, and at the
same time, the reality before us challenges our beliefs. At
such times, the prayer of the hopeful father - "I believe.
Lord help my unbelief!" (Mk 9:24)- is my prayer, too.*

*Act like you know what you're doing
and most people will believe it.*

WHERE GOD'S FLOWERS BLOSSOM

The place is a real mess –
A down-right mell of a hess.
The raw cinder block walls
Surround these halls
Of skeletal buildings
With their rusted gildings

The ground is rough, broken
Pools of old oil a token
Of work that once was done
By men since gone
On rotting yellow hulks –
Machines that now sit, sulk

This is Camp Suicide;
Zaidan, Iraq sits astride
Some secondary roads
That carry loads
From one sad backwater
To another, hotter

It's an ugly old place
Wearing an uglier face
That poverty and war
Together mar;
North of the Euphrates,
A half step from Hades

There, amid this rubble,
God blew a kind of bubble
Stark in this ravished land.
From God's own hand
Purple flowers blossom.
Stunning, simply awesome.

Transfixed, I stop and stare
At this crown bejeweled there –
A monument to life
Within our strife.
Hope, a moment at least,
Then return to the beast.

Rockets explode nearby
So I tear away my eye
And head for the bunker
Where we hunker
Down, down close to the dirt –
A call; someone is hurt.

But memory retains
An image without such stains
Of broken bodies, blood,
Oil, sweat, and mud.
Once there was a garden –
West. Remember Eden?

Will I return some day
And with my family stay?
Or will my next flowers
Be grave towers
Sitting in a basket
By a gilded casket?

Don't know. There's work to do.
From rainbow's purple hue,
Move to opposing red –
A brother's dead.
Sad effects of slaughter
Sent to loving daughter.

This place is a real mess –
A down-right mell of a hess
Of broken bodies, blood,
Oil, sweat, and mud
Where God's flowers blossom.
Stunning, simply awesome.

*****

*I pondered a beautiful, flowering bush in the middle of
our camp, set up in the rubble of a site once used to
maintain equipment for the irrigation system along the
Euphrates southwest of Baghdad on one of the routes to
Fallujah.*

The primary purpose of a plan is to have a base from which to deviate.
Plan on deviating.

STILL THERE

I'm awoken by the call at midnight
"An IED on the roadside hit one of our patrols
Casualties are inbound, let's roll."
Pull on my boots, tie 'em up tight
Thanking God this ain't every night.

We await what comes, listen for rockets –
Screaming, gauze wrapped 'round his head,
                            the gunner's first to arrive.
At least we know he's still alive
Though bits of shrapnel cast pockets
Of shadow from bloodied sockets

That the docs have something to do grabs me
And they start doing it–their waiting's done, it's all over–
But I've got nothing, no cover
The screaming continues, stabs me
Helplessness angers, maddens me.

Finally, I'm able to stop and breathe.
The anguished cries subside as his mates
                            bring the next one in.
Bright white teeth make a grisly grin
Though everything above those teeth –
Gory jello, his brain unsheathed.

That night – it's been over a decade since.
Screaming echoes, reverberates, bounces with my tears,
While toothsome grin shines through the years
Desperate, I want to make sense,
Box the pain with intelligence.

I can't and I'm bound to that summer fright.
God! I don't want to forget, and don't want to remember,
Heart's stuck; don't know what to pray for
Do you even hear me this night?
Reach into darkness, make it right!

Think of those men, their families, in prayer
I'm back in the hut in Mahmudiyah, in dark and dust
Though all the rest is long since rust
Still I look to God. Do you care?
Because I'm still helpless, still there.

*****

The incident happened in August 2004. It is, perhaps, one of the most vivid images of that time to remain with me. I don't get worn out with flashbacks, but there are some pictures we never get out of our minds.

The authority to point out what's wrong entails the responsibility to point out what's right.

EVENING PRAYER

Three bells. 2130. Time to go.
Across the passageway, down the ladder,
Through the hatch out into the hangar bay
Dodging the low-slung wings of the fighters
As I to starboard make my quiet way.

There's a long line aft at the smoking head;
Shadows that snake and curve in the red light.
Through hangar doors, reflecting off the crests
Of waves rolling by, bright sparks of moonlight
Burst and fade on soft, brilliant, foamy nests.

Another hatch, then start the long slow climb.
On the way up, I pass by the skipper,
Then one more ladder and I'm at the bridge.
Declare myself: "Permission to enter?"
Traditions reach out, bind us, stitch by stitch

In the muted stillness, greet the bo's'n,
Take my station by the 1MC where
Four bells sound. 2200. Then pipe
"All hands, stand by for evening prayer"
Read a psalm, say a prayer – you know the type:

"Now I lay me down to sleep,
I pray thee Lord my soul to keep.
Watch those who watch throughout this night
And bring us safe to morning light. Amen."

I linger just a little on the bridge –
Maybe step outside to the weather deck,
Or talk with the bo's'n, or stand silent,
Peering into the space 'tween black and black
Of deep, dark sky at night and ink-toned sea.

More often I go up the ladder aft,
Find the weathered chair on the signal bridge,
Relax and talk to the quartermasters
Debating which constellation is which
And what it all means, these stars upon stars.

I drift off to another place and time
Where other chaplains stood beneath the stars
As bo's'ns piped the ship to ev'ning prayer.
The sails billowing above hard-worked tars,
While yardarms creak and new, young middies stare.

In our modern age, it's almost a curse,
The honored past and this word "tradition."
But on a night like this, it's like the weight
Of a blanket, comfortable, and warm –
Cocooned, I enter in that blessed state.

Six bells. 2300. I retire.
Snug in my stateroom, that sweet, sweet bastion,
I pull this tradition up to my chin.
Another day underway is fin'lly done
And e'er the seventh bell sounds, I'm all in.

*****

*My favorite part of the day – evening prayer, then aft on
the signal bridge, staring up at the stars. Such a blessed,
archaic tradition.*

Outside of America, "new" is not often considered a good thing.

SHOES

I join the Ops-O out on the fantail,
Looking into the darkness over the water.
The noise and bustle has paused
And we stand silent, as anxious fathers.

"There are all sorts of hazards out there,"
He says grimly. "Things that will tear out a boat's keel."
He just sent the ship's boats out.
We wait, flinching at each radio squeal.

Young people, out in the looming dark
Searching, searching desperately for survivors:
Gulf Air Flight 72
A few moments ago hit the water.

How hard it is to stay back in safety
While sending our children away into danger
Then seeing them return, changed –
Searing pain engraved by mangled strangers.

In their eyes is where I see it first –
Angry, haunted, pleading, hoping, despairing eyes.
What did they see in the dark?
What lies beneath their mangled, stifled cries?

69

Wreckage, yes, and torn, shredded bodies,
But what hurt most were things
                    that didn't make the news –
Looters sifting through corpses,
Souvenirs from last vacations, and shoes.

Shoes – little shoes, bobbing up and down
Beside little feet that will not wear them again,
Bump up against the gunwale –
Toddlers in pieces, knocking, "Let me in."

The young officer is nearly frantic
"I have to stand my watch. I have to. I have to!"
He needs to do, dares not think
Of teddy bears and tiny feet and shoes.

As he tells me what he saw, I see
Shoes and feet and teddy bears swimming in his tears.
I hear his heart in pieces
Knocking, begging, pleading, "Will someone hear?"

A fatherly embrace, I tell him
"You did well, son. I'm proud. You did your duty well.
Come back after watch is done.
We'll face the demons, though we wade through hell."

He leaves, relieved; he will stand his watch.
On the fantail, I note the sun's first dawning hues.
As waves lap against the hull,
I hear the children looking for their shoes.

*****

I was on board the USS GEORGE WASHINGTON (CVN 73) in August of 2000. We were getting ready to leave the port of Manama, Bahrain, when Gulf Air Flight 72 crashed on approach, killing all 143 people on board. We were tasked with recovery operations over the next 48 hours and for the next 72 hours afterwards I was busy with critical incident debriefing. Almost all of the young people mentioned the looters and the shoes. The older officers spoke of the worry they had sending sailors about the same age as their own children out into those dangerous waters. All of us were changed.

Just because God has a plan doesn't

mean you don't need one.

SEVENTEEN AND EXPECTED
(NOW THAT IT'S ME)

Got the email 11 July
"This morning, your Dad died."
It was kind of expected
After 17 years with MS.

I stared at the screen of the laptop
Pondering what I ought
To do with this sort of news
Now that it's me, not the troops.

Emergency leave is the standard
When one's deployed and your
Family back home gets hit
With a loved one dying like this.

I told the XO I wasn't sure
If I would head homeward
Then the Skipper came down
Not much inclined to hear me out.

He cut off my "yeah but's" and "what if's"
And said, "I'll settle this.
You're going home, that's an order.
You'll not make your mom a martyr."

So off I went, first down to Kuwait
Then to Paris – delayed –
But First Class into the States
And a rental in the lot waits.

Got the email on 16 July
"This morning, Bryan died."
It was kind of expected
After 17 weeks in Iraq.

I stared at the screen of the laptop
Pondering what I ought
To do with this sort of news
Now that it's me and my troops.

*****

I went home on emergency leave when my Dad died after a long struggle with Multiple Sclerosis in 2004. The first email I received when I got home was a note from my RP that one of my Marines had been killed. The weight of death hit me hard, and the desire to be in both places at once broke my heart - one of the most difficult days in my life.

74

You can't dance with the Devil and
expect to just walk away.

GOOD FRIDAY, 2004

A runner sent
On summons bent -
The veil is rent
And there my duty lies

A long black bag,
A plain beige tag,
A bloody rag,
Point where my duty lies

No surgeon's balm,
Echoes a psalm
Riven heart calm
For here my duty lies

Prayers for the dead,
So quickly said -
The men he led
Are where my duty lies.

*****

Good Friday, 2004, was when we took the first two KIAs in our battalion.

Evil is not explained in the Bible.

Explanations are excuses and evil

must never be excused.

IN AND OUT

In and out, in and out, in and out –
Can you just go already?
In and out, in and out, in and out –
I need something more steady.

In and out, in and out, in and out –
Children round me patter.
In and out, in and out, in and out –
Do I look like your father?

In and out, in and out, in and out –
Rules constantly changing.
In and out, in and out, in and out –
Home always re-arranging.

In and out, in and out, in and out –
Never know where I'm at.
In and out, in and out, in and out –
It's not a ship, it's a cat.

In and out, in and out, in and out –
Really, I do love you.
In and out, in and out, in and out –
Please know that the kids do, too.

In and out, in and out, in and out –
But we need you to go
In and out, in and out, in and out –
Put an end to "to and fro"

In and out, in and out, in and out –
Bring on this six month bout
In and out, in and out, in and out –
Then when you're out, you stay out

In and out, in and out, in and out –
But when at last you're back
In and out, in and out, in and out –
Then we can get our lives on track.

*****

Perhaps the most difficult part of being married to a sailor is not the regular deployment, but the work-ups to that deployment. Out with the ship for a week, in port for a weekend, out for a day or two, back in for a week, and on it goes. And every time I left or returned, the routine changed. For those two years, the phrase our kids heard most often was either, "Do I look like your mother?" or "Do I look like your father?"

If you have to tell me you're in charge, you're not.

TOO HOT AND A COT

I sit on the edge of a cot.
My boots are off, and also socks,
Because it's noon and bloody hot –
Heat radiating from the rocks.

I drink lots of lukewarm water
That flows from pores like tiny springs
And just seems to make me hotter;
A crust of salt around me rings.

We hear it coming, hit the deck –
Kaboom! That one is way too close!
Another hits, my RP checks;
But all I think of are bare toes.

Heedless of my bodyguard's shout,
I hobble off to get my boots
Before I head to our dugout
To sit, silent, like budding roots.

These rocket attacks are a bitch
And I sure resent donning boots
Because my feet still ache and itch
From several weeks' warm abuse.

A call comes on the radio
"Man down!" We head to BAS.
A round hits near, but still we go
Making our way through this hot mess.

Things like that make me stop and think
That nearby round was just a dud
I didn't stop or even blink
So close I came to spilling blood.

Why was I spared, not even scratched?
Gunny the other day got dead.
He has little kids, barely hatched
A whistle, boom, and no more dad.

Our mortars are returning fire
I find our wounded man is fine
Later, back on my cot and tired
Still too hot, Gunny on my mind.

****

It's hard to convey just how great the pleasure is, after so much time in the heat and dust and dirt to just have my feet exposed to the air - and thus, how much I resented having to reshod.

And it's hard to convey just how great the pleasure of knowing a man like Gunny B. and having him around to make that heat and dust and dirt a little more bearable - and how much I resent losing him.

We are answerable to *God*, not the other way 'round.

FAITH

How do you know it's God?
No. Really.
How do you know?

Just one little bullet
It misses me,
So I say "Thank God"
But one little bullet
Kills another.
Do I then blame God?

It could have been worse
So it's a miracle.
Should have been better
So why does God hate me?
Is God the ultimate politician
Taking credit for the good,
Blaming others for the bad?

Or is it all a big gamble?
You make your choice,
You place your bets.
You roll the dice.
Sometimes the dice
Come up craps.

My father told me
At my brother's grave
"Never underestimate
The power of God
To redeem."

To redeem.

I've seen redemption.
I've seen craps win the game.
I've seen death inspire life.
I've seen evil bring justice.
I've seen muck turn into flowers.
I don't understand it.
I can't answer my questions.
But I will hope in
The power of God
To redeem.

****

I believe in divine providence and predestination. I also believe in a God who used the instrument of human evil – the unjust execution of an innocent man – to bring about the salvation of the world. And I don't understand it.

Don't try to pretend you're perfect in front of God. He knows better.

VIETNAM VETS

Old men gather
To remember
When they were young
And stood so tall
Despite it all
Life but a song
To sing out loud
For they were proud
Of being called
To serve their land
To take a stand
To risk it all

They remember
These who gather
Those who paid it
And didn't come
With the rest home
The dust they bit
"Never forget"
We try, and yet
Never is long
Years roll on by
And tears do dry
As youth is gone

But still they gather
And remember
The prisoners
And MIAs
Full fare they paid
On foreign dirt
So when they meet
To see and greet
Those who remain
They see it still
The bloody kill
Again, again

Stooped they carry
The memory
Haunt the nation
That would forget
And shun regret
To vacation
They won't let us
Escape from this
Bright dream that died
In rice paddies
Where these laddies
Fought, bled, and cried

They will gather
And remember
What they did for
God and country
'Neath canopy
Of jungle war
Now folks thank 'em
Try to shelve 'em
On dusty racks
Where none will see
This memory
Upon their backs

But that's okay
Folks are that way
These remember
Who lives, who's dead
What they all did
When they gather
To honor those
Who never rose
To come on home
But still stand tall
Despite it all
To those that know

Face the dog.

"What are we supposed to do with all this God-damned stuff?"

OTHER POEMS

GENERATIONS

My grandfather was a preacher,
But I never knew him.
He grew up in Sheboygan
Then died out in Lynden.

His son thought he would try teaching
But didn't go direct.
First he went down to the sea
In uniform bedecked.

I remember a day when I
Was only 5 years old,
Walking with him on the pier;
Gray ships tied up, stark and bold.

I thought, "I want to go to sea
On warships great and gray –
Sail out on the water,
With bows cutting through salt spray."

I worked hard to be a sailor,
But couldn't go direct.
I had to go preaching
Before I could stand on deck.

Finally, my God let me go
To sea on board a ship –
A huge, mighty vessel
That between the deeps did slip.

The vast, dark waters below us,
The vast, dark sky above;
A million dots of light
Sifting through them like a sieve.

Time has passed now and I'm on shore.
My heart remains at sea,
Striving o'er cresting waves.
One last voyage will I see.

But now my sons are off to sea,
Children of proud fathers.
And out 'tween sea and sky,
The generations gather.

*****

*In May 2015, my youngest son graduated from the Naval
Academy and I was privileged to put new ensign
shoulder-boards on him. My older son is in the Navy
Reserve and considering whether God has called him to
the priesthood. In my sons, the heritage of preacher,
teacher, and sailor combine again as the old is made new.*

We do not thank the hammer, but the carpenter.

DARE BE A DAD

It's all over.
It's just begun.
Holding this child,
First time ever,
I feel real dumb.

I got this far;
Now what to do?
Dare be a dad.
Can I to her?
Visions race through –

What if I mar
By explaining
The facts of life;
Maybe leave scars
Potty training?

This is scary
As I ponder
Holding this child
Kind of hairy
As I wonder

But I'm this far,
Have to do it –
Dare be a dad.
Try to lead her,
Muddle through it.

*****

*I remember well the feelings I had that day towards the
end of May in 1988 when my daughter was born and I
held her for the first time. The wonder, the joy, the fear –
all ran through my heart and head. Here I was,
responsible for this helpless human being, and I know just
what an idiot I can be. God help her with a dad like me.*

All the people I've met who claim to be atheists aren't. They're just really mad at God.

FIRST CHURCH

The church says I can be a pastor
But first I need a place where
A pastor is sufficiently needed,
Else that promise goes unheeded.

I've lived in big cities and small towns
Cars, trains, and crowds make the sounds
I've grown up with and fallen asleep to
As summer nights prepare for dew.

The elder calls to ask three questions:
Would you come if we beckon?
Do you have children? We would like to know.
And can your wife play the piano?

I told them the truth – yes, yes, and no.
And figured we'd never go
To the small church in Hull, North Dakota:
No piano means no Dakota.

Hull doesn't even rate a map dot –
A tiny, isolated spot
About four miles off US 83
In the middle of endless prairie

Just ten houses, a church, and some barns
Where farmers retire, spin yarns
Of days and men now faded and long gone
When ev'ry heifer calved more than one.

There used to be a gas station here
Gone now, but an old slab bears
Witness to the industry that once marked
Former lives and hopes now decades dark'ed

Progress has not been good for this place
But that's okay – folks like space;
And the kids found work – Bismarck – nearby.
Besides, not much point to asking why.

Like the winds that rise and fall across
The open sky need no cause,
It just is, and we just are, and we
Need a pastor. Would you please be he?

*****

*I'm basically a city boy. I've lived in small towns a few
times, but mostly small to moderate sized cities. So when
I was called to Hull, ND - a town of 9 occupied houses,
one abandoned house, a church, and some barns between
the Missouri River and US 83 - I went with some
trepidation. I was there four years and they were four
good years. They're used to breaking in newly minted
pastors and they were gentle with me and my mistakes. I
left when I joined the Navy in 1995.*

The object of work is the work itself.
Enjoy that. God will see that it
achieves something.

WANDERING THE WILDERNESS

Before I was born, my father left Egypt,
His wife expecting their first child.
Out into the wilderness they went
By Providence light, to Athens, count the miles!
Then further, away to the east,
Wandering out through the windswept wilds.

Later, I was born in that wild wilderness
As father sought the Promised Land.
I think, at last, he may have found it –
He is dead now, his discovery in hand.
But I'm still out here wandering
Over windswept sea and endless sand.

In its way, it's beautiful, magnificent,
Carved and whittled by God's own hand.
Multihued towers, stunning blossoms –
Against wondrous backgrounds, posed, they stand,
Sweep my breath away in glory!
Yet I still long for the Promised Land.

It's been a great adventure and I've seen much –
Beclouded pillars backed by sun;
Colossal waves dancing in the wind;
Towers of fire leaping forth from the mountain;
Endless sky on a bed of grass –
But there's still one place I've never been.

In all my wandering, Canaan still eludes
I'm not even sure where it is.
Would I recognize it? I don't know.
Maybe it's just a dream and doesn't exist.
Maybe there is no Promised Land –
Just earth, sky – a vast, wide nothingness.

No, there must be a Promised Land out somewhere,
A place to call home there for me,
A place where I'm not a visitor,
A place where I belong and can freely be,
Not a role or a title or job –
Just plain old me, whatever they see.

And I think my dad may, at long last, have found it
After his years in the wilderness,
After his struggles and his stumbles.
So I'll wander 'till I find it, too, I guess –
Keep looking for the Promised Land
Out somewhere beyond the emptiness.

*****

*I've lived in in 12 different states and one foreign country
– an average of not quite 4 years per home state. In
addition, I struggle (as many do) with questions of
vocation, of caring for a loved one with a chronic illness,
and of the purpose and meaning of it all. I heard
someone tell me once too often that God has a plan to
bring us home. Great. Then let's make it happen because
I'm sick of the Wilderness. I want the Promised Land.*

Semper Gumby

HOME

"Where's home?"
Home...
How do I answer that?

An address?
Just a spot on a map.
Not home.

"What's home?"
Home...
How do I answer that?

A town?
Just a name for the spot.
Not home.

"Who's home?"
Home...
Yes. I can answer that.

She is.
My wife, my love, my life –
Home.

*****

*In my travels, moves, and changes of employment, I often
get asked the question: "Where's home?"*

I'm glad you didn't mean to. You must also mean not to.

HEADING TO A COUNTRY CHURCH

Heading down the two lane,
Clouds are overhead,
Pressed against the glass;
Blue sky framing the pane.

I drive, navigate past
Corn standing tall
In neat, ordered lives
And beans in low, squat nests.

A façade – all a show
That hides the dirt
And covers over
The chaos down below.

Up ahead, like pillars,
Beams of light strike
Through the breaking clouds;
Sloughs away the filler.

I'm told it all depends
On what you are,
Maybe who you are,
Before the story ends.

But I've no time to search,
So past the nests
And neat, ordered corn
I make my way to church.

*****

*I sometimes get asked to preach in nearby churches and,
as my life is a bit higgledy-piggledy right now, it struck
me how neat and clean it sometimes appears in church,
when we're really heading along in a fog hoping for a
little light to clear things up.*

Direction is more important than distance.

SPIRIT MOUND

Clouds stretch, spike, and roll
Like an EKG
Heartbeat of the world
Against a blue scroll

Mild day for August
Following the trail
Through milkweed overhang
Breeze stirring the dust

Birds sing in the grass
Insects resonate
Joyful prairie choir
Sounds as we file past

Climbing to the top
I see roads and fields –
Civilization –
But here it all stops

I try to picture
Before surveyors
And the mapmakers
Brought their strictures

When undivided whole
Through infinite space
Spread in its glory
Confounding my soul

Can't make sense of it
I find I need lines
To cut the world to
Manageable bits

But I stop, wonder
Is this how God is
Sans theology
To break asunder

Spirit tied to ground
Tries contemplating
His infinity
From this little mound

*****

My wife enjoys walking up to the top of the Spirit Mound here in South Dakota. The last time we were there, I was struck by the way we need to break up earth, sky, and even God into small bits in order to digest. Infinity is frightening.

Pain is a very effective teacher.

WAITING FOR THE BAT BOY

Waiting on the Lord
I'll renew my strength, I'm told.
It's there, in the word
But this waiting's gettin' old.

The Lord will provide –
I really do believe that.
Still feel cast aside
Like a baseball player's bat.

Against the backstop,
Blending with the backfield dust
Haphazardly drop't –
I've got some use left – I must.

Waiting for the boy
To come running and fetch me,
To be re-employ'd
And challenge this world's pitching.

It seems forever
Though I'm sure the boy's running.
He won't leave me here.
I'll wait. He must be coming.

*****

*It's was over a year after I stepped aside from my position
as senior pastor before I found other work. Waiting and
trying to discern how and where I should serve next is
hard. I hold to the promises of God - they've never failed
me yet - but waiting is hard.*

Make a decision and trust God.

THE WORSHIP SERVICE

From opening gun the announcer speaks,
The crowd on its feet, eager, anticipating.
Noise rises - tumultuous, like unto song;
And the Word is... "You're off!"
Passing peppermints, the people said, "Amen."
"By the way, who won?"

*****

*I wrote this one in seminary when in a cynical mood
regarding worship and worship planning. Sometimes it
still feels this way.*

It's not your job to be better than him.
Your job is to be better than you.

CRIBBAGE LIFE

Four
Hot chocolate?
-teen
Suppose so.
Fifteen for two
I'll set the water to boil
Twenty
No worries. Your turn.
Thirty
Marshmallows?
Thirty-one for two
No. That's okay.
Four
Too hot for you?
-teen – one for last card.
I'll get to it soon.

Nine
I'm leaving for Germany.
Fifteen for two
How long?
Twenty-one for two
All summer.
Thirty for one
What will you be doing?
Eight
Missing you, I think.
-teen
I think I'll miss you, too.
Twenty-five
Marry me when I get back?
Thirty-one for two
Have to think about that.

Six
How was your day?
Twelve for two
Not bad. I guess. Okay.
Fifteen for two
Something wrong?
Eighteen for two
No. Not really.
Twenty-seven
Then what's up?
Thirty-one for two
Think I'm pregnant
Three
Pregnant? Like, pregnant?
Eight
Like, pregnant.

Seven
We leave in March
Fifteen for two
Where to?
Twenty-four for three
Iraq. Seven months.
Thirty for four.
They need you there.
Thirty-one for two
Yeah. They do.
Seven
We'll be waiting.
Fifteen for two
I'm sure I'll be back.
Twenty-one for three.
I know you will.

*****

My wife and I started seeing each other regularly to play cribbage and, at first, that's all either of us had in mind. Since then, cribbage has accompanied all the ups and downs of the 33 years since we first sat down to play. This is just a little taste.

Don't go looking for trouble – it'll find you without any help.

CHURCH QUESTIONS

Heard anything?
How's it going?
Find anything?

No.
Fine.
Not yet.

Week after week
Same questions
And same answers

Heard anything?
How's it going?
Find anything?

No.
Fine.
Not yet.

They are concerned
And curious
And want to know

Heard anything?
How's it going?
Find anything?

No.
Fine.
Not yet.

I am concerned
And curious
And want to know

Heard anything?
How's it going?
Find anything?

Maybe skip church
So I can
Skip the answers

*****

*I know the questions arise out of a genuine concern for
me. These people have been and continue to pray for me
as I look to find what comes next for me. I am grateful for
the prayers and the concern. But it is hard to go to
church and have the same questions posed by 20-30
people, if not more, every bloody week.*

Prayer is not a "honey-do" list for God.

THE VOICE

Trembling, I stand on the threshold
Peering into the murky depths beyond.
Fear and fascination
    Mix
        Mingle
            Become entwined within me.

Out of the swirling darkness,
A voice shines forth
A stabbing, searing light
    Flickering
        Fading
            Fragmenting my mind.

Stirring thoughts, long forgotten.
Rising from the abyss,
Images dance on the words,
    Thrusting
        Twirling
            Retreating to a silent music.

And still the voice probes on,
Asking forbidden questions
Seeking answers I do not have
   Questions
      Challenges
         Demands confound me.

A light shining in the darkness
Revealing neglected corners
That I would hide
   Gaining
      Growing
         Guiding where I fear to go

Terrified, I cry out
"God save me!"

"I am."

*****

I wrote this initially in response to the feelings generated while working with a young lady suffering from Multiple Personality Disorder.

I'm still breathing, so it's a good day.

Made in the USA
Columbia, SC
15 January 2018